UNDERSEA UNIVERSITY

The Fish Files

by
Jonathan Kronstadt

with **Mary Cerullo**
Consultant

SCHOLASTIC INC.

New York Toronto London Auckland Sydney
Mexico City New Delhi Hong Kong Buenos Aires

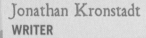

Jonathan Kronstadt
WRITER

Jonathan writes about science, nature, and sports for children and adults. He lives with his family in Silver Spring, Maryland. He's been following fish with his mask and snorkel since he was a kid, and has seen everything from a barracuda to an electric eel. Shocking!

Mary Cerullo
CONSULTANT

Mary has been teaching and writing about the ocean for thirty years. She lives in Maine and works as the associate director of Friends of Casco Bay, an organization that protects and studies the bay.

ISBN: 0-439-71185-1

Copyright © 2005 by Scholastic Inc.

Illustrators: Yancey C. Labat, Ed Shems

Photos:
Front cover: (panda butterflyfish) Georgette Douwma/Photographer's Choice/Getty Images; (ribbon eel) Stephen Frink/Imagebank/Getty Images; (monkfish) Ken Lucas/Visuals Unlimited; (wrasse) Mike Kelly/Imagebank/Getty Images.
Back cover: (puffer) Marty Snyderman/Visuals Unlimited; (oriental sweetlips) Georgette Douwma/Imagebank/Getty Images.

Page 5: Tim Flach/Stone/Getty Images. Page 8: (top) D.W. Miller; (lamprey) Patrice Ceisel/Visuals Unlimited; (hagfish) Christine Ortlepp. Page 9: (top) Richard Herrmann/SeaPics.com; (denticles) Dr. Dennis Kunkel/Visuals Unlimited; (whale shark) David Fleetham; (stingray) Hal Beral/Visuals Unlimited. Page 10: (parrotfish) James Gritz/Photodisc/Getty Images; (scales) image100/Getty Images; (sunfish) Stephen Frink/CORBIS. Page 11: (sea star) Dr. James P. McVey/NOAA Sea Grant Program; (mollusk) Digital Vision/Getty Images; (jelly) Michael Aw/Photodisc/Getty Images. Pages 12 and 48: (gills) Phillip Colla/SeaPics.com. Page 15: (sawfish and catfish) John G. Shedd/Visuals Unlimited.
Page 16: (cusk eel) Marty Snyderman/Visuals Unlimited; (weakfish) Tom McHugh/Photo Researchers; (black drum) Shedd Aquarium/Ceisel/SeaPics.com. Page 18: (bluefin tuna) Richard Herrmann/Visuals Unlimited; (blue marlin) Masa Ushioda/SeaPics.com; (sailfish) Doug Perrine/SeaPics.com. Page 21: (swordfish) Franco Banfi/SeaPics.com; (barracuda, puffer, and eel) Marty Snyderman/Visuals Unlimited; (flounder) Daniel Gotshall/Visuals Unlimited; (butterfly fish) Reinhard Dirschel/Visuals Unlimited. Page 22: (flounder) Chris Huxley/Taxi/Getty Images; (halibut) Marty Snyderman/Visuals Unlimited. Page 23: (kingfish) Richard Herrmann/SeaPics.com; (herring) Aldo Brando/Stone/Getty Images. Pages 23 and 48: (fish 1) David Wrobel/Visuals Unlimited; (fish 2) John C. Lewis/SeaPics.com; (fish 3) James D. Watt/SeaPics.com; (fish 4) Franco Banfi/SeaPics.com. Page 24: (pipefish) Mark Conlin/SeaPics.com; (flatworm) Marc Chamberlain/SeaPics.com; (sweetlips) Robert F. Myers/SeaPics.com; (snake eel) Tom McHugh/Photo Researchers; (sea snake) Ron & Valerie Taylor/SeaPics.com. Page 25: (stonefish and butterfly fish) Marty Snyderman/Visuals Unlimited; (frogfish) Steven Norvich/Visuals Unlimited; (blenny) Franco Banfi/SeaPics.com; (cleaner fish) Mark Conlin/SeaPics.com. Page 26: (clown fish) CORBIS; (Achilles tang) Doug Perrine/SeaPics.com; (lionfish) Andrea Menotti. Page 27: (porcupine fish) Dean & Sharon Williams/SeaPics.com; (stingray) Phillip Colla/SeaPics.com; (surgeonfish) Robert Myers/Visuals Unlimited; (boxfish) Doug Perrine/SeaPics.com. Page 28: (sea devil) E. Widder/HBOI/Visuals Unlimited; (flashlight fish) Ken Lucas/Visuals Unlimited; (black sea dragon) Doc White/SeaPics.com; (viperfish) Gregory Ochocki/SeaPics.com. Page 29: (swordfish) Eleonora de Sabata/SeaPics.com; (butterfly fish) Ken Lucas/Visuals Unlimited; (sea horse) Bill Kamin/Visuals Unlimited; (lumpfish) Reinhard Dirschel/Visuals Unlimited. Page 32: (school) Richard Herrmann/Visuals Unlimited. Page 34: CORBIS. Page 35: Doug Perrine/SeaPics.com.
Page 36: OAR/National Undersea Research Program/NOAA. Page 39: CORBIS. Page 40: Donald Flescher/Marine Biological Laboratory. Page 41: (top) courtesy of Dr. Andy Rosenberg; (herring) Doug Perrine/SeaPics.com. Page 42: (Chinook salmon) Brandon Cole/Visuals Unlimited; (bluefin tuna) marinethemes.com/Kelvin Aitken. Page 43: (silver eel) Doug Stamm/SeaPics.com; (monkfish) Espen Rekdal/SeaPics.com; (blue shark) Richard Herrmann/Visuals Unlimited. Pages 42–43 and 48: (map) NASA/R. Stöckli/Robert Simmon/GSFC/MODIS. Page 44: (mudskipper) Brian Rogers/Visuals Unlimited; (archer fish) Stephen Dalton/Photo Researchers; (parrotfish) Marty Snyderman/Visuals Unlimited. Page 45: photos courtesy of Dr. Robert Warner. Page 47: (A) James D. Watt/SeaPics.com; (B) Norbert Wu/www.norbertwu.com; (C) Bill Harrigan/SeaPics.com; (D) Reinhard Dirschel/Visuals Unlimited; (E) Marc Chamberlain/SeaPics.com; (F) Tom McHugh/Photo Researchers; (G) Doug Perrine/SeaPics.com; (H) Marty Snyderman/Visuals Unlimited; (I) Brandon Cole/Visuals Unlimited.

12 11 10 9 8 7   6 7 8 9/0

Printed in the U.S.A.
First Scholastic printing, January 2005

The publisher has made every effort to ensure that the activities in this book are safe when done as instructed.
Adults should provide guidance and supervision whenever the activity requires.

Table of Contents

page 30

There's Something Fishy

So, ocean explorer, would you believe there are fish with armor? How about fish with suction cups? Fish with *light-up whiskers*? Well, guess what—you're about to meet all of these fish and more!

This month's Undersea U adventure will be a treat for your eyes and your imagination as you discover just how amazing fish can be. Along the way, you'll find the answers to all sorts of questions, like:

- What makes a fish a fish?

- How do fish breathe?

- Do fish sleep?

- How do fish stay afloat?

- How do fish catch food?

- How do fish keep from *becoming* food?

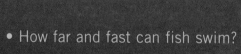

- How far and fast can fish swim?

- Which fish is the biggest?

- Do fish talk?

You'll get the scoop on sharks, the facts about flounder, tales about fish scales, and so much more. Get ready to dive in and meet all sorts of fantastic fish face-to-face!

Going On—

How Fish Go with the Flow

Fish have to ace all kinds of survival tests if they're going to make it in the undersea world. Fortunately, fish get all A's when it comes to *adaptation*. Adaptation is a long word that means changing what you do to help you survive. Adaptation happens slowly, over millions of years, as fish find better and better ways to avoid their predators, to feed themselves, and to handle other life-or-death challenges.

Fish can adapt by developing:

- **special coloring** to hide from predators or prey.

- **body parts** that can protect them and help them get food, like spikes, stingers, body armor, and more.

- a **body shape** that helps them swim fast to avoid predators, or a **body size** that's too big to swallow!

And those are just a *few* of the ways fish can adapt. Fish are so good at surviving that they make up more than half of all the species of *vertebrates* (that's animals with backbones) in the world—there are about 25,000 different species of fish!

Fantastic Fish—On File!

As you flip through the pages of this book, you'll meet some of the wildest—and weirdest—fish in the seas. They're positively fish-tastic! Look for them featured on Fish Files like these:

FLASHLIGHT FISH

Lives in: Indian Ocean, Red Sea

Cool fish feature: Flashlight fish light up to attract to blink signals to follow flashlight fish, and the predators. Not surprisingly, they're nocturnal, which means they're more active at night. Who needs a flashlight during the day?

What's in This Month's Undersea Kit?

This month, you'll become a full-fledged fish designer with Undersea U's Make-Your-Own Fish Kit. The kit includes sixty-seven assorted fish parts—heads, tails, bodies, fins, and more—that you can use to create your own brand-new fish species!

You'll find all sorts of fish design challenges in **Part 3: Survival of the Fishest**—see if you can create a fish that'll survive in the darkest depths…a fish that can hide in a colorful coral reef…a fish that can outswim its predators in the open sea…and much more! This book will give you all the fish facts you need to make your fish design choices. Just add your imagination, and—voilà!—your fish are born!

Make-Your-Own Fish Kit
You've got sixty-seven fish parts—and some of them glow in the dark!

The Undersea University Website

For more fish fun, surf over to **www.scholastic.com/undersea**, where you'll be able to design more of your own fish online! You'll need this month's password to dive in (you'll find it on the right). Make sure to log in soon!

WEB-SURFING PASSWORD

GOFISH

PART I

Fish Fundamentals

So You Wanna Be a Fish?

If you want to be a fish, there are certain things you must have. What are they? Take a peek at Clarence Clearfish below—he's got 'em all.

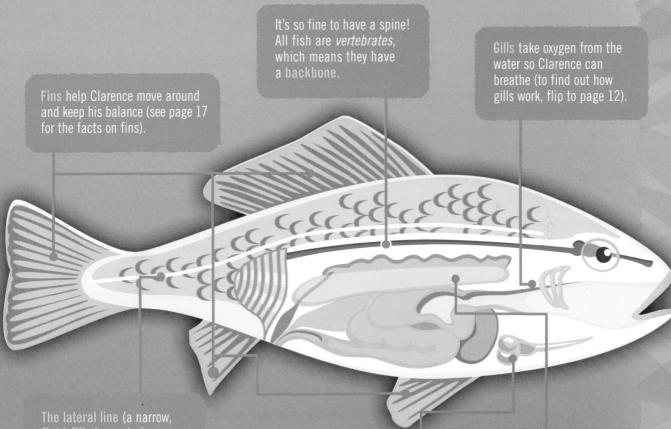

It's so fine to have a spine! All fish are *vertebrates*, which means they have a backbone.

Gills take oxygen from the water so Clarence can breathe (to find out how gills work, flip to page 12).

Fins help Clarence move around and keep his balance (see page 17 for the facts on fins).

The lateral line (a narrow, fluid-filled canal along Clarence's side) helps Clarence detect vibrations in the water, which makes it easier for him to find food, avoid predators, and generally get around smoothly (see page 15 for the lowdown on lateral lines).

Clarence is cold-blooded, which means his body temperature will most often be the same as the water he swims in.

Clarence has a swim bladder that helps him stay afloat—it has air inside to keep him from sinking. However, unlike all the other parts on this page, this is not a required fish part. Most fish have these, but not the fish you'll meet on page 9!

The First Fish

About 500 million years ago—long before dinosaurs were around—the first fish appeared in the seas. They were slow swimmers; they had no jaws; and they were covered with bony plates. They weren't exactly beautiful, but they *were* the first animals to have backbones.

bony plate

no jaw

This is an artist's drawing based on the earliest complete fossil of a fish.

Look Ma, No Jaws!

Some jawless fish are still around—check out the files below to meet two of them! Other species of fish eventually developed jaws, and now there are two main types of jawed fish—**cartilaginous** and **bony**—which you'll find on the next two pages.

LAMPREY

Lives in: Rivers and coastal seas

Cool fish features: Lampreys latch onto other fish and suck their blood for nourishment! They can also suck up small invertebrates (animals without backbones). Lampreys are born in rivers, spend some time as adults in the sea, and then return to rivers to lay their eggs and die.

This is the lamprey's head—the rest of it looks like a big worm.

HAGFISH

Lives in: Chilly waters on the seafloor

Cool fish features: Hagfish can do a neat trick— they can tie their worm-like bodies into knots! Hagfish also ooze out slime to ward off predators—and then slide their bodies into a knot to clean the slime off.

Imagine Us—Cartilaginous!

Tap the tip of your nose—notice how it's squishy? That's because it's made of *cartilage*, just like the skeletons of about 350 species of sharks, rays, and other *cartilaginous fish*. These types of fish have been around for about 400 million years! Here's a quick list of what makes them special:

They have five or more **uncovered gill openings** on each side. Most other fish have a single opening for their gills, covered by a bony flap.

Their mouths are stocked with **multiple rows of teeth**, which can move forward when a front tooth is lost.

They have **no swim bladder**, so if they stop swimming, they start to sink! Fortunately, it doesn't take a shark much effort to stay on the move—their bodies are streamlined to move through water easily.

Instead of scales, they've got **tough skin** made of *denticles*—tiny toothlike spines that protect the fish from injury.

They're equipped with **electricity detectors** called *ampullae of Lorenzini*, which are bundles of cells on their heads that enable them to sense weak electric fields produced by other fish. That's how sharks find prey buried in sand on the ocean floor. So don't play hide-and-seek with a shark— even if it's willing to count to 100!

WHALE SHARK

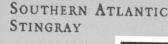

Lives in:
Warm waters near the equator

Cool fish features:
Whale sharks are the biggest fish in the world, topping out at 46 feet (14 m) long and 30,000 pounds (13,600 kg)! Even though they're sharks, they don't eat like most other sharks—they eat microscopic plankton and other tiny creatures by filtering 1,500 gallons (5,700 liters) of water an hour through their gill rakers (see page 12 for more on gill rakers).

SOUTHERN ATLANTIC STINGRAY

Lives in:
The Atlantic, from New Jersey to Brazil

Cool fish features:
These bottom dwellers are shaped liked diamonds, with "wings" that they flap to swim. Unlike most fish, stingrays give birth to live young instead of eggs.

No Baloney...
We're Bony!

Bony fish must be doing *something* right, because about 97 times out of 100 when you see a species of fish in salt water, it's a bony fish. The earliest bony fish (from about 400 million years ago) had lungs that allowed them to breathe out of the water for very short periods. Some bony fish species evolved into lung-breathing, land-living amphibians (frogs, toads, salamanders, and more), while the rest stayed full-time in the seas.

Here are a few things all bony fish have in common:

- **Skeletons** made of bone (surprise, surprise!)

- **Covered gills** on the sides of their heads

- **Swim bladders**, which keep them from sinking when they stop swimming (see page 13 for more on this)

- **Scales** covering their bodies, for protection from bumps, bruises, and scrapes.

covered
gills

overlapping scales

OCEAN SUNFISH

Lives in: Oceans all over the world

Cool fish features:
The ocean sunfish is the world's biggest bony fish— it grows up to 11 feet (3.4 m) long and can weigh 3,000 pounds (1,360 kg). Sunfish love to eat jellies. They also like to lounge near the ocean surface for warmth.

Fish Scales Tell Tales

mini Quest

Fish and trees don't have much in common—except growth rings! Scientists can tell how old fish are by looking at the growth rings on fish scales. Some fish scales, like the one shown on the right, have a pattern of rings that represent their growth over seasons. Rings grow far apart in the spring and summer, and closer together in the fall and winter. One set of close-together rings combined with one set of far-apart rings equals one year.

See if you can tell how old this fish is! You can check your answer on page 48.

Why Can't We Be Fish?

Some animals have fish in their names but not in their bodies. Starfish, jellyfish, and shellfish aren't fish (they have no backbones!). So please call them sea stars, jellies, and mollusks.

Dolphins and whales live and swim alongside fish, but actually they're *mammals* like us. They have lungs instead of gills, which means they have to come to the surface to breathe. Like other mammals, they're warm-blooded and give birth to live young.

NOT fish...

sea stars

mollusks

jellies

dolphins

...also NOT fish!

whales

PART 2:
How Fish Work

So, ocean explorer, do you want to know how fish breathe? How they float and swim? How they see, hear, feel, smell, and taste? Then you've come to the right part of the book! We'll start with the big question...

How Do Gills Work?

Fish need oxygen, so fish need gills. These magical membranes allow fish to suck oxygen right out of the water. Gills work this way:

1

The fish opens its mouth to take in water.

2

The fish closes its mouth and pushes the water past its gills, which have feathery folds (called *lamellae*) covered with blood vessels. The lamellae absorb oxygen from the water.

3

The gill cover opens to allow water (and carbon dioxide, which fish exhale just like we do) to flow out.

More Gill Thrills

How's this for weird? Some fish use *hooks* to catch food. They're called gill rakers, and they're little bony hooks or spikes that latch onto tiny creatures (or other types of food in the water) as water flows through the gills.

gill rakers

Test Your Gill Skills

See if you can identify gill parts in the fish below. Check your answers on page 48!

1) lamellae   2) gill cover   3) gill rakers

mini Quest

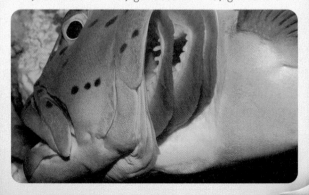

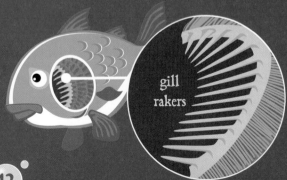

Sink or Swim

What You Need

- Clear plastic pitcher (or a 2-liter soda bottle with the top cut off)
- Water
- Film canister
- Pennies
- Vegetable oil

Having a swim bladder makes every fish gladder, because otherwise they'd have to swim forever—or sink! Swim bladders are like balloons that fish can inflate or deflate as needed to stay afloat without having to swim. Try this Sea Quest to see how swim bladders work.

swim bladder

What You Do

Part 1: Making Cents of Swim Bladders

For a fish, getting just the right amount of air in its swim bladder is the key to staying at just the right level underwater. Too much air, and the fish would float to the surface. Too little air, and the fish would sink. See if you can find just the right combination of air and weight to make your film-canister fish hover underwater!

film canister

1. Fill the plastic pitcher with water almost to the top.

2. Put the film canister into the water. Guess what—it floats!

3. Now take the film canister out and add a penny to it. Click the lid back on and lower the canister back into the pitcher. Shake the canister underwater to get rid of bubbles that might be trapped underneath it, then let go.

4. Does your canister still float? If so, keep adding pennies one at a time. How many pennies can your canister hold without sinking to the bottom? Can you find just the right number of pennies to make your canister hover in the middle of the water?

Check out **Sea the Point** on the next page to find out how your canister compares to a real fish swim bladder!

pennies

Part 2: Oil's Well That Floats Well

What happens when a fish doesn't have a swim bladder? That's the case with *cartilaginous* fish (flip back to page 9 if you haven't already met them). These fish use oil in their livers to help them stay afloat. See how that works by trying this quick demonstration.

1. Put two pennies in the film canister, close it, and drop it into the water. Like a fish with a swim bladder full of air, it floats!

2. Now fill the film canister with water, keeping the pennies inside. Like a fish with an empty swim bladder, the canister sinks.

3. Empty the water out of the film canister, but keep the pennies inside. Now fill the canister with oil and drop it into the water. What happens? Does the oil make the canister float?

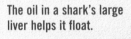

The oil in a shark's large liver helps it float.

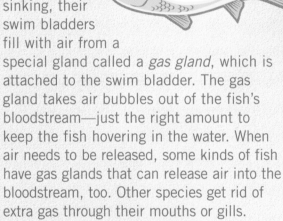

liver

Sea the Point?

In Part 1, the canister played the role of a fish's swim bladder. When you added pennies, you were adding weight and removing air, so the canister sank lower, as a fish does when it lets air out of its swim bladder.

You probably had a tough time getting the film canister to hover between the top and the bottom of your pitcher. That's because the balance between rising and sinking is very delicate. But fish are able to balance themselves in water with ease, thanks to their swim bladders!

Here's how fish do it: If they need to become lighter to avoid sinking, their swim bladders fill with air from a special gland called a *gas gland*, which is attached to the swim bladder. The gas gland takes air bubbles out of the fish's bloodstream—just the right amount to keep the fish hovering in the water. When air needs to be released, some kinds of fish have gas glands that can release air into the bloodstream, too. Other species get rid of extra gas through their mouths or gills.

swim bladder

In Part 2, you should have found that your film canister floated when you filled it with oil. This is because oil is lighter than water. Since sharks have no swim bladders, they store large quantities of oil in their livers to keep from sinking.

Sea Senses

Fish senses are—in a *sense*—like human senses. But they can be wildly different, too. If we take them one by one, you'll see what's the same, and what isn't.

SIGHT

Fish eyes work a lot like human eyes, but they're much better at seeing in dark and murky undersea conditions.

SMELL

Like you, fish have nostrils on either side of their snouts. Some fish use their sense of smell to detect food and nearby predators.

TASTE

Fish have taste buds not only inside their mouths, but also on their heads, fins, bodies, tails, and even whiskers (if they have any). Having taste buds spread out all over allows a fish to taste the bitterness of a poisonous fish without actually eating it.

HEARING

Fish have ears, but you can't see them. Sound vibrations travel from the water through the fish's body to its internal ears.

TOUCH

The lateral line (found on each side of all fish) is the closest thing that fish have to a sense of touch. These lines are fluid-filled canals lined with tiny sensing "hairs." The hairs detect vibrations in the water around them, sort of like when you feel the wind brush against your cheek (you have tiny hairs there, too!). Fish use this sense to stay with their schools, to find mates and food, and to sense when predators are coming.

Downright Sense-sational!
Check out the senses on these watery wonders!

SAWFISH

Lives in: Shallow coastal waters of tropical seas

Cool fish features: Sawfish have special receptors on their snouts that enable them to sense the heartbeats of creatures buried in the ocean floor. Then they use their snouts to slash away at their prey.

CATFISH

Lives in: Salt and fresh water just about everywhere

Cool fish features: Catfish have taste buds all over their whiskers, bodies, fins, and tails—there are up to 27,000 taste buds on a single fish (your tongue has less than half that many). Since catfish have such a good sense of taste all over their bodies, some people say they're like giant swimming tongues!

sawfish

Underwater Clatter!

You might think it's quiet underwater, but if you listen very closely, you just might hear...A WHOLE LOT OF NOISE! Actually, you wouldn't hear *everything* that goes on, as some fish sounds aren't made for human ears. But more than 500 species of fish worldwide can sound off when they want to, and they want to for the same basic reason we want to: to get noticed! Here are just a few of the coolest marine musicians:

WEAKFISH

Lives in: The Atlantic, from Canada to Florida

Cool fish features: Weakfish make a purring sound by contracting the muscles around their swim bladders. In schools, they make noise that sounds a lot like the static you get when a radio station is not tuned in.

CUSK EEL

Lives in: Warm and tropical waters everywhere

Cool fish features: Cusk eels use a special bone in their spines as a drumstick to bang on their swim bladders (because they're filled with air, swim bladders are kind of like drums!). Cusk eels are noisiest when looking for a mate, especially around sunset.

cusk eel

BLACK DRUM

Lives in: The Atlantic, from New England to South America, and the Gulf of Mexico

Cool fish features: These fish are named for the noise they make by banging their muscles against their swim bladders. They make this noise to get noticed when they approach their egg-laying grounds and want to attract a mate.

black drum

Want to hear the real deal when it comes to fish music?

Go to www.scholastic.com/undersea and you'll get an earful! Just make sure to bring along this month's password, found on page 6.

Fun with Fins

Without fins, being a fish would be a real floppy experience. You'd be at the mercy of ocean currents, and you'd probably spend much of your life upside down or sideways. To find out how fins work, check out old Clarence below—he's got all the fin facts!

Top fin (dorsal fin) This fin is used primarily for balance and steering. Some fish have more than one. Some have sharp spines in their dorsal fins to protect against predators. In some fish, this fin has evolved into a long lure that attracts prey (see page 28).

Tail fin (caudal fin) The tail fin moves a fish forward, like the motor on a boat. Its shape tells you a lot about its owner. The fastest fish have forked or crescent-shaped tail fins (find out why on page 18).

Bottom fins These fins help keep Clarence from rolling over. Some fish have adapted these fins to latch on to the seafloor (see page 46).

Side fins (pectoral fins) These may be the hardest-working fins on a fish's body. They help fish swim faster, swim slower, turn left and right, go up and down, and keep from rolling over. To slow down, fish fan their side fins out to catch water and act like brakes. To speed up, fish draw their side fins close to their bodies to reduce drag. Some fish even use their side fins to swim backward!

Swim Systems

Fish swim under the waves by making waves of their own. They start their S-shaped waves by moving their heads from side to side. As the wave moves down their bodies, it gets stronger and grows larger, ending at their tails, which swing widely back and forth. This wave pushes water sideways and backward, which makes fish move forward.

PART 3:
Survival of the Fishest!

To survive under the sea, fish have two very important jobs: Avoid anything that wants to eat them *and* find their own food while they're at it! Not *every* fish has what it takes—only the strong survive. In this section, you'll explore all the ways fish have found to stick around, and by the end you'll know enough to design your own super-survivor fish!

Speeding Through the Seas

For some fish, speed is the key to survival. These undersea speed demons zoom through the ocean to escape from predators and catch prey. Over time, some species have developed the supreme shape for swiftness. A streamlined body that's narrow and pointed at each end—like a torpedo—is best. And the tails of fast fish are usually forked or crescent-shaped. Why this shape? Well, when fish swim, they swing their tails from side to side—and if the tail is broad and flat, water can't get around the tail when it's out to the side. This slows the fish down. But water can easily flow around forked and crescent-shaped tails, letting the fish really fly!

SAILFISH

Lives in: Open waters of the Atlantic and Pacific Oceans

Cool fish features: The world's fastest fish, sailfish have been clocked at up to 68 miles per hour (109 km/h). That's faster than a cheetah can run! The sailfish maximizes its speed by lowering its top fin into a groove on its back (groovy idea!).

BLUE MARLIN

Lives in: Atlantic and Pacific Oceans

Cool fish features: In the oceans, bigger doesn't necessarily mean slower, and the blue marlin is a perfect example. Blue marlins weigh up to 1,200 pounds (544 kg) but are one of the world's fastest fish, reaching speeds of 50 miles per hour (80 km/h).

BLUEFIN TUNA

Lives in: Atlantic and Pacific Oceans mostly, but warm waters everywhere

Cool fish features: These speedsters can swim up to 45 miles per hour (72 km/h), and can cross the entire Atlantic Ocean in less than sixty days. They can live up to forty years.

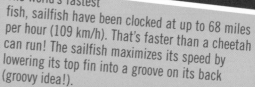

bluefin tuna

Shape Up
and Go!

If you want to move fast, you have to get in shape, right? That's definitely true for *people*. But for *fish* who want to be speed demons, it's not so much about being *in* good shape—it's about being *a* good shape. Take on this Sea Quest, and you'll discover why some fish bodies are built for speed!

What You Need

- Long shallow baking dish
- Water
- Scissors
- Cardboard
- Bar of soap

Your Crew

- Adult adviser to help cut soap
- Friend to race against

What You Do

1. Fill the dish with water, almost to the top.

2. Cut the cardboard into three pieces: one circle, one rectangle, and one pointed teardrop, each about 2 inches (5 cm) long. These are your "fish."

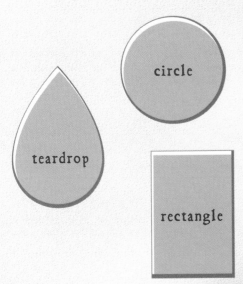

circle

teardrop

rectangle

3. Cut a little V-shaped slit into the back of each fish as shown below.

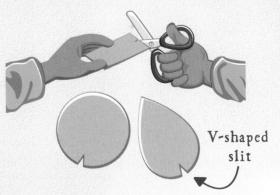

V-shaped slit

4. Ask an adult to cut three little slivers of soap for you.

5. Wedge the soap slivers into the slits on each fish.

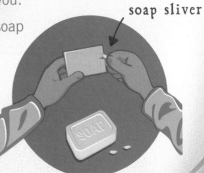

soap sliver

6. With a friend's help, drop all three cardboard fish in the water at the same time. You should see the fish move across the dish! This is because the soap in the back creates a slimy film that allows the cardboard to glide through the water (if you want to know why, check out the box below).

7. Which fish moves the fastest? Try the race a few times (with fresh water each time), and see if you get a clear winner!

Sea the Point?

Did you notice that the pointed teardrop moved faster than the other fish? It should have. The teardrop's point allows it to cut through the water. The circle and rectangle have more surface area for the water to latch onto and slow them down.

The heads of streamlined fish are pointed like the front of your teardrop shape, while slow-swimming fish have rounded heads like the circle. There's even a box-shaped fish like your rectangle—you guessed it, it's a slow fish, too. Check out the chart on the next page for more on fish forms!

The Soap's the Secret!

Wondering what made your cardboard fish move forward? It's because of a force called *surface tension*, which is created by water molecules pulling toward each other on the water surface. If you drop a piece of plain cardboard onto the water, the water molecules that are pulling toward each other will tug slightly at the edges of the cardboard. If they tug equally on all sides, the cardboard won't move.

Soap has the power to break the surface tension of water.

In this Sea Quest, you added soap to one side of your cardboard fish. The soap's sliminess broke the water's surface tension at the back of the fish, so the water was no longer tugging back there—but it *was* still pulling at the front. This let your fish glide forward!

Shape Up for Survival

Fish shape affects fish speed, as you saw in the previous Sea Quest. But fish come in all shapes, and each shape helps the fish survive. Check out the chart below to get the facts on fish forms!

Shape	How It Helps the Fish Survive	Who Has It
Fusiform	The fusiform (streamlined) shape is widest in the middle and narrows to a point at each end of the fish. This shape allows fish like the swordfish to speed long distances through the water chasing after prey.	swordfish
Rod	This body shape is perfect for predators who lie still for long periods of time waiting for prey, then streak out of their hiding place to attack quickly. These fish, like the barracuda, specialize in short bursts of speed.	barracuda
Depressed	These fish aren't sad—the name "depressed" in this case means *flat*. Being flat allows fish like the flounder to hide on the seafloor.	flounder
Sphere	Having a big round shape makes it very hard for a predator to get its mouth around these fish! Sphere-shaped fish like the puffer can suck in enough water (or air, if it's at the surface) to quadruple in size in just a few seconds.	puffer
Ribbon	Ribbon-shaped fish like eels can slither between rocks and into crevices both to find food and to hide from predators.	eel
Compressed	Compressed fish (flat on both sides) like the butterfly fish are shaped just right for making quick, sharp turns and for slipping into cracks to hide from predators or to get at food that other fish can't reach.	butterfly fish

Undersea
Hide and Seek

Predators can't eat what predators can't find, so one of the best ways to avoid becoming *see*-food is to blend in with your surroundings. This tricky technique is called *camouflage*, and you'll find some real *out-of-sight* examples on these two pages!

Now You See Me...Now You Don't!

For some fish, changing colors is a downright brilliant way to stay alive. These fish have cells full of color—called *chromatophores* (KROH-ma-toh-fors)—in their skin. By stretching and shrinking these cells, the fish can change their colors to blend in with their surroundings.

HALIBUT

Lives in: Atlantic and Pacific Oceans

Cool fish features: The biggest of the flatfish, halibut can grow up to 700 pounds (318 kg). But even the biggest can still change color when camouflage is called for. They do a great job of matching the colors of the sand on the seafloor.

This peacock flounder is colored to blend in with the ocean floor.

Shady Characters

Fish that use countershading—a light color on their underbellies and a darker color on top—are tough to see from above and below. Just ask the yellowtail kingfish on the right!

Atlantic herring also use countershading to help avoid predators.

YELLOWTAIL KINGFISH

Lives in: Cool waters around the world

Cool fish features: These cleverly colored kingfish are hard to see from above, since their bluish green tops help them blend in with the dark ocean below. But they're also hard to see from below, because their light-colored bellies blend in with the brightness of the ocean surface. Tricky, huh?

Find That Fish!

It's a camouflage contest! There's a fish hiding out in each of these pictures. See if you can find them without consulting your local ichthyologist (that's a fish specialist). Then turn to page 48 to see if you were right.

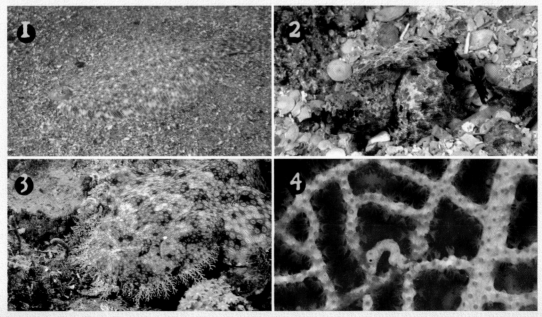

Masters of

Camouflage is definitely a great way to stay out of sight (and out of stomach)—but wait till you see *these* tricky disguise tactics!

Copycat? Copyfish!

Some sneaky fish look like leaves and grass—stuff that definitely wouldn't be on a predator's lunch menu! Check out the pipefish on the right.

Scare Tactics!

Not all disguises are so innocent—below you'll find two fish designed to make predators go YIKES!

PIPEFISH

Lives in: Oceans all over the world

Cool fish features: Pipefish do a fabulous job imitating a single blade of grass, and since there are no cows or goats underwater, they can escape getting eaten this way.

terrible-tasting flatworm

JUVENILE CLOWN SWEETLIPS

Lives in: Indian Ocean

Cool fish features: The small, defenseless juvenile clown sweetlips looks and swims like a type of flatworm that tastes terrible and makes fish that eat them feel even worse.

HARLEQUIN SNAKE EEL

harmless snake eel

Lives in: Indian and Pacific Oceans

Cool fish features: The harlequin snake eel is a peaceful, harmless sort of fish, and it would be a tasty target for predators—if the snake eel didn't look so much like the highly poisonous banded sea snake. Even hungry predators won't take that kind of chance.

defenseless fish

poisonous sea snake

Fish-guise!

Trick AND Treat!

The art of looking like something you're not—or *mimicry*—isn't just used for protection. Predators can get in on that game, too! Some devious predators use mimicry to look harmless right until the moment they swallow their unsuspecting prey.

STONEFISH

Lives in: Coral reefs

Cool fish features: Stonefish have pieces of skin hanging off their bodies that make them look like seaweed-covered rocks, letting them snatch unsuspecting prey. And the thirteen poison-filled spines on their backs keep predators at bay.

FROGFISH

antenna

Lives in: Indian and Pacific Oceans

Cool fish features: Frogfish can change colors to look like rocks or coral. Then, the frogfish wiggles a long antenna on its head to make it look like a small, easy-to-eat fish. When another fish comes in to dine, it becomes dinner instead.

SABER-TOOTHED BLENNY

pretends to be harmless

Lives in: Indian and Pacific Oceans

Cool fish features: Maybe the craftiest copycat of them all, the saber-toothed blenny looks, swims, and even does the same underwater dance as the cleaner fish, which eats parasites and dead skin off other fish, keeping them clean and healthy. But when a fish approaches this blenny for a cleaning, it gets a chunk bitten out of its flesh instead. And before the wounded fish can react, the blenny speeds away.

Eye Can't See You

If you thought copycatting was cool, fish have plenty more tricks—like using fake eyes to give predators the slip!

This four-eye butterfly fish has just two eyes—but the fake ones on either side of its tail fool predators into thinking the butterfly fish is facing the opposite direction. When the predator approaches the wrong end, the butterfly fish makes its escape!

← harmless cleaner fish

BEWARE! I'm Poisonous!

So, now you know that fish can hide in lots of ways to avoid becoming sea snacks. Well, now it's U-turn time: Some fish have colors and patterns that scream "Look at me!" for the very same reason. These bright fish are flashing warning signs to any predator who might think a snack is in sight. The message is loud and clear: "I'm dangerous—so stay back if you want to live past lunch!"

Color Me Yucky

Eating these brightly-colored fish would not be such a bright idea for a hungry predator....

CLOWN FISH

Lives in: Tropical waters around the world

Cool fish features: Clown fish aren't poisonous themselves, but they hang out among the poisonous tentacles of sea anemones, protected by a layer of mucous that covers their bodies. The clown fish's bright bands of color alert predators not to come near unless they want to get stung by the anemone.

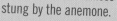

clown fish

ACHILLES TANG

Lives in: Tropical waters of the Pacific Ocean

Cool fish features: The Achilles tang has a bright orange spot near the base of its tail that calls attention to the razor-sharp spine in the middle of the spot. You can see it here as a thin dark line—the spine is sticking out toward you.

sharp spine

LIONFISH

Lives in: Indian, Pacific, and Atlantic Oceans

Cool fish features: The lionfish is anything but subtle. In case you miss the huge, poisonous spikes sticking out of its body, it has zebra-like stripes in a bunch of different colors to get your attention.

Spikes, Spines, and Stingers
(Oh My!)

Since getting eaten can really ruin your day, fish have found many methods of staying out of predators' stomachs. Some of them involve being downright unswallowable. Check out these well-armed defenders:

porcupine fish

STINGRAY

Lives in: Oceans all over the world

Cool fish features: Stingrays carry barbs on their tails that are up to a foot long. Their barbs can produce pretty big stab wounds, and they can also inject a dangerous poison. Fortunately, stingrays aren't aggressive, earning the nickname "pussycats of the sea." They'll only strike when threatened—or stepped on (they rest on the sandy seafloor).

PORCUPINE FISH

Lives in: Tropical waters all over the world

Cool fish features: Porcupine fish are covered in sharp spines and can puff up to unswallowable sizes, so even *starving* predators steer clear of them. Porcupine fish are devastating on offense, too, with jaws strong enough to crack open the shells of small ocean creatures like sea urchins—that would be like you cracking a coconut with your teeth!

SURGEONFISH

Lives in: Coral reefs all over the world

Cool fish features: Surgeonfish are well named, with spines near their tail that cut like a surgeon's scalpel. There are seventy-five species of surgeonfish, and all can slash predators with their spines when threatened, leaving a lasting—and bloody—impression.

The sharp spine is hard to see because it blends in with the surgeonfish's stripes. In this photo, it's sticking out toward you.

BOXFISH

Lives in: Coral reefs in the Pacific Ocean

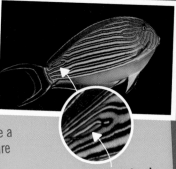

Cool fish features: Ever wonder what it's like to eat a tuna fish sandwich without opening the can first? Try taking a big bite out of a boxfish and you'll get a pretty good idea. Boxfish are protected by a triangular box of bony armor—and if that doesn't discourage you, they respond to stress by releasing a highly toxic poison.

A Light Bite

I magine you're an innocent young fish, swimming in a deep, dark ocean. You see what appears to be a light up ahead. Do you:

A) Get curious and decide to swim toward the pretty light

B) GET AWAY!

Cooooool!

If you picked **B**, congratulations, young fish—you get to live! Some of the nastiest-looking, most ferocious feeders in salt water use pretty lights to attract prey. Check out a few of them below!

the sea devil's lure

TRIPLEWART SEA DEVIL

Lives in: Atlantic, Indian, and Pacific oceans

Cool fish features: The triplewart sea devil is a type of anglerfish. The word "angler" means *fisher*, and that's exactly what this fish does—with a glow-in-the-dark lure! The sea devil dangles the lure in front of its head and flashes the light—then waits for its prey to swim right up to its mouth. What a bright idea!

FLASHLIGHT FISH

Lives in: Indian Ocean, Red Sea

Cool fish features: Flashlight fish light up to attract food, to blink signals to fellow flashlight fish, and to confuse predators. Not surprisingly, they're nocturnal, which means they're more active at night. Who needs a flashlight during the day?

BLACK SEA DRAGON

Lives in: Atlantic, Indian, and Pacific Oceans

Cool fish features: Black sea dragons have whiskers that light up to attract prey. They also have red lights under their eyes that they can flash to communicate with other black sea dragons.

light-up whisker

VIPERFISH

Lives in: All the world's oceans

Cool fish features: The viperfish may be the scariest fish to ever glow in the dark. Viperfish swim thousands of feet below the surface—where it's very dark—and flash lights on and off all over their bodies. When a fish swims by to catch the light show, the viperfish attacks with fangs so big they don't even fit in its own mouth. To eat extra big fish, the viperfish can even unhinge its jaw.

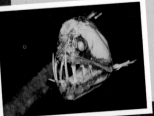

Fine Dining, Fish Style

When it comes to chowing down, fish have all sorts of ways of getting food into their bellies—and you can often tell how they get their food just by looking at their mouths! Here are two fish with mouths just right for their preferred dining methods.

SWORDFISH

Lives in: Oceans all over the world

Cool fish features: Billfish like this swordfish use their sharp bills to slash fish in schools, then swallow the dead and wounded ones.

LONG-NOSE BUTTERFLY FISH

Lives in: Tropical waters of the Pacific Ocean

Cool fish features: These fish poke their long noses into the cracks and crevices of coral reefs to get at food hiding inside.

Stay Put!

Some fish don't like to hunt for their food—they sit and wait. But staying in one place underwater isn't as easy as it sounds! That's why the fish below have special body parts to help them stay put under the sea while they wait for a meal.

SEA HORSE

Lives in: Oceans just about everywhere

Cool fish features: Sea horses have tails that they can wrap around things like blades of sea grass and coral. This helps keep them from being bounced around by ocean currents while they're trying to catch food. Then they use their mouths like tiny straws to slurp up zooplankton.

LUMPFISH

Lives in: Coastal waters of the North Atlantic

Cool fish features: Lumpfish must be the laziest feeders in salt water. These slow swimmers use a suction cup on the bottom of their bodies to attach themselves to rocks, then wait for food to come to them. Sound like anyone you know?

the lumpfish's suction cup

Make Your Own Fish!

So, ocean explorer, now that you're an expert on all kinds of fishy facts, it's time to grab your Make-Your-Own Fish Kit and start designing your own swimming sensations! With sixty-seven fish parts at your disposal, you'll be able to make all kinds of aquatic wonders.

Maybe you'll build a super-fast fish with huge fangs and a poison-spiked tail? Maybe you'll design a glow-in-the-dark eel that can glide through murky underwater caves? It's totally up to you! All you need is your imagination, the fish expertise you've picked up so far, and the assembly instructions on these two pages!

Your Make-Your-Own Fish Kit includes:

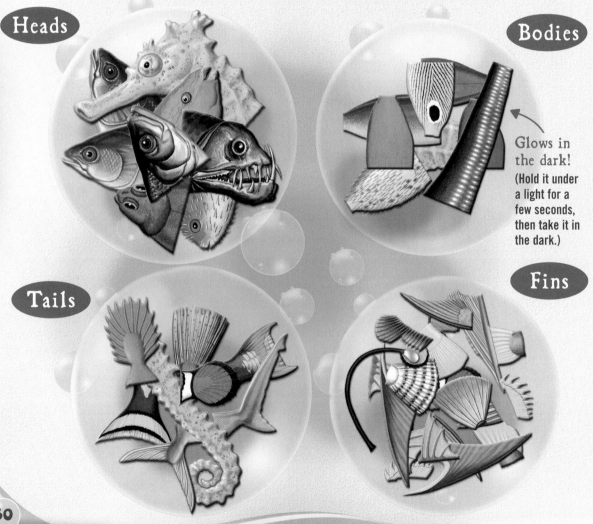

Heads

Bodies

Glows in
the dark!
(Hold it under
a light for a
few seconds,
then take it in
the dark.)

Tails

Fins

What You Do

1. Grab a body, a head, and a tail from your kit. Pick any ones you want—no need to match colors!

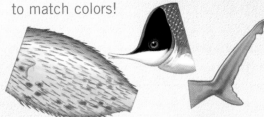

2. Take one of the circle connectors and attach it to the head.

3. Slide the body into the other end of the connector.

4. Attach the tail to the body using another circle connector.

5. Now you have your basic fish, but wait—how is your fish going to steer and slow down (and generally keep from flopping over in the water)? You'll need some side fins for that! To attach side fins, grab two side connectors (one of each kind, as shown above). Then slide one connector onto each of the side fins.

hole   plug

6. Stick both side fin connectors into the hole in your fish's body and press until the connectors snap together.

7. Now decide what other fins your fish will have. Will your fish have spines? A shark-style fin? How about a special kind of fin that looks like an antenna (but is really a glow-in-the-dark fishing rod)? Whatever you decide, use a circle connector to attach the fin (or *fins*)!

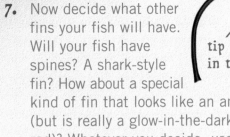
tip glows in the dark

8. When your fish is done, attach a circle connector to the bottom and slide the connector onto one of the cardboard stands. Then stick the stand into the base, and your creation is ready for display. Give your fish a nice official-sounding fish name, too, like the fangmouth glowfish...or the flatface bottomslider...or the purple poison puffyhead!

9. You have enough parts and stands to build five fish at a time, so let your imagination go wild! (Then take your fish apart and start again!)

Survive in Style!

Okay, fish designer, it's time to get cracking! On the next few pages, you'll be given a series of seagoing challenges, and you'll be in charge of building a fish that can survive each situation. When you're done, check out some solutions on pages 37–38 to find out if your fish would be a survivor!

Out in the

Welcome to the open ocean, fish designer! We're far from shore, where the water's deep, the predators are big and fast, and the hiding places are few. Dive into the following dilemmas and see if you can build fish to handle each one! You can check your designs on pages 37–38.

1 When Speed Is What You Need

▶ **The Challenge:** You need to stay on the move all the time to chase after your lunch, and you also need to avoid *becoming* lunch for speedy predators! What's the answer? Think fast!

▶ **Make It!** Build a streamlined fish that can speed through the oceans.

2 Quick, Hide! Yikes, Where?

▶ **The Challenge:** With hungry predators lurking above and below, you need to find a good way to stay out of sight. But there's nowhere to hide! What can you do to keep from being seen?

▶ **Make It!** Design a fish that can conceal itself in the open ocean.

3 When Being Yummy Is Deadly, Be Yucky Instead

▶ **The Challenge:** If you don't have speed on your side, you need another way to make predators steer clear. Being poisonous is a great idea! But your defense will only work if you can somehow let your predators know you're bad news *before* they polish you off.

▶ **Make It!** Make a fish that's clearly a bad-news bite—one that predators will just pass by.

Open Ocean

4 ## So Many Fish, So Little Time

▶ **The Challenge:** A school of fish passes by and you're getting hungry. But if you try to snatch the fish away one at a time, the school will be long gone before you've have time to eat your fill. How can you nab several fish before you miss your chance?

▶ **Make It!** Make a fish that can attack a whole school of fish, injuring or killing many at once. (Hint: Your fish needs a body part that it can use as a weapon!)

Cruisin' Around the Coral Reef

Now that you've mastered the challenges of the open ocean, it's time to move on to the busy, colorful world of coral reefs. See if you can fashion some fish that'll live well in the reef!

⑤ Eye Spy

▶ **The Challenge:** Your food is hiding just beyond your reach inside crevices in the coral reef, and you need some way to get it. Plus, you need to stay safe from predators who lurk around the reef, trying to sneak up and eat you.

▶ **Make It!** Make a fish that can poke around for food in tiny spaces AND make sudden getaways that'll really surprise predators!

⑥ Cozy Crevices and Hiding Holes

▶ **The Challenge:** You can't blend in with the coral reef scenery, but you need to hide somehow. What's a fish to do?

▶ **Make It!** Make a fish that can slip into the cracks and crevices of a coral reef and maneuver around them in search of food.

Found in warm ocean waters, coral reefs might look like plants, but they're actually hard structures created by tiny animals called corals. When corals die, the skeletons they leave behind form reefs. Coral reefs provide food and shelter for thousands of fish species and plenty of other sea animals—they're like

Make Your Own Fish!

Life's No Bore on the Ocean Floor

The ocean floor can be a busy place. It can be sandy, muddy, or rocky, and it can support a wide variety of life. But it can also be dangerous, because predators know there's food down there, and in shallow waters the currents can toss you tail over fins. Try your hand at creating some fish that can survive on the seafloor.

⑦ I'm Just Hanging Around

▶ **The Challenge:** You need a way to keep from being bounced around by the coastal currents so you can eat (and hide) in peace!

▶ **Make It!** Make a fish that can hold still when the water's thrashing!

⑧ Why Is the Floor Moving?

▶ **The Challenge:** You're very tasty, not very fast, and too big to slip into a crack anywhere. Your best bet is to hide on the ocean floor—but you need to keep your eyes on everything that's going on overhead!

▶ **Make It!** Make a fish that won't be seen on the ocean floor, but can still see anything else that swims by.

Deep, Dark, and Downright Daunting

$\mathbf{T}$here are a few good reasons why there isn't a lot of life in the deepest parts of the world's oceans. It's dark...it's cold...there's not much to eat, and the weight of all that water above creates unbearable pressure. To survive down there takes some very special sea skills, and for those who have them, it's a truly wild world. Can you make some fish that can face the ultimate challenge?

9 Will Somebody Please Turn On a Light?

▶ **The Challenge:** You can't eat what you can't see, and you can't see a thing down here.

▶ **Make It!** Make a fish that can create its own light to find food deep down in the ocean.

10 Here, Fishy Fishy

▶ **The Challenge:** It's hard to search for food when the water's nearly pitch black. If only there was some way to get your prey to come to *you*!

▶ **Make It!** Make a fish that can lure in its prey!

Along some of the deepest parts of the ocean floor lie *black smokers*—vents in the seafloor that gush out hot mineral-rich water.

How'd You Do?

The Undersea University Department of Fish Engineering has taken on the same challenges you faced on pages 32–36, and they've put together some out-of-this-world fish. Take a look at the fish they've created to survive in each of these environments, and find out if *your* fish have what it takes.

1. Fast and Forked

There's no way you'll catch up to the hastyfish. Your fish needs a streamlined body (widest in the center and pointed at each end) and a forked tail. If it's got these parts, you survived this challenge!

2. Hiding from Top to Bottom

The invisifish blends in from above and below. As long as your fish was *countershaded*—darker on top and lighter on the bottom—you survived this challenge!

3. A Bad Bite

The spikefish is one miserable mouthful—and any predator who sees it knows that. If your fish was brightly colored and covered in spikes, you survived!

4. Three Strikes and You've Got Lunch

The slashfish gets its food by striking a school of fish with its long, sharp nose, then eating the dead or injured ones left behind. As long as your fish had some kind of body part that could slash or strike, you tackled this design challenge!

5. Just Poking Around

The which-way fish fools its predators by making them think its head is actually its tail. It also has a mouth shaped just right for poking around in coral to find food. If your fish had a spot like an eye near its tail and a mouth that's long and thin, you have a winner!

6. Slipping In for a Snack

The sleek and slimy slitherfish knows the ins and outs of reefs all over the world. As long as your fish was long and narrow, you can chalk it up as a survival star!

7. Hold On Tight

The grabberfish has a tail that holds on to plants while it eats, keeping the tides from sending it topsy-turvy. As long as your fish had this kind of tail, you passed this survival test!

8. Things Are Looking Up

Odds are you won't see the flat-as-a-pancake fish no matter how hard you look, as it can just about disappear into the brownish ocean floor. But with both eyes on top of its head, it's likely to see *you*. If your fish was flat, brown, and had eyes on top of its head, then you aced this challenge!

9. Lighting It Up Below

The flashfish can find food even in the ocean's darkest depths. As long as your fish had a glowing body, you passed with glowing colors!

10. Going Fishing

The danglefish lures in its prey with a light it dangles in front of it. As long as your fish had the glow-in-the-dark antenna, you survived!

Congrats, fish designer! Your fish-fashioning skills have really been put to the test! For more fish-making fun, make sure to visit **www.scholastic.com/undersea**!

PART 4:

Fish on the Move

By now, you know that fish have two basic goals: finding things to eat, and avoiding things that want to eat *them*. You've seen fish adapt in amazing ways, making them real experts when it comes to survival—but even so, sometimes their best move is just to stay in school!

Safety in Numbers

About 80 percent of the world's fish species swim in schools (or large groups) at some point in their lives, and it's easy to see why. It's much harder for predators to single out just one fish when there are thousands swimming together, looking like one huge fish. Schools also help make sure plenty of fish eggs hatch, because a school lays massive amounts of eggs—more than predators can eat. Schools are also useful for hunting, since it's much easier to attack prey with the help of a few thousand friends!

School All Day Long?

Do fish stay in their schools around the clock? Nope—many schools break up at night, and each fish finds its own place to sleep. You might not know a sleeping fish if you saw one, though, because they don't close their eyes (they can't—they have no eyelids). Check out page 44 to see a sleeping fish!

Staying in School

What's truly amazing is the ability of fish in schools to move together in a totally coordinated way. Fish can instantly detect movements of their schoolmates, and a school of thousands of fish can almost move as one.

A fish knows what the rest of its school is doing by using its keen vision, its lateral line (which helps it detect movement nearby), and tightly packed bundles of hairs called *neuromasts* that stick out around its head and body, helping it sense motion.

Scientists have also found that fish schools create currents in the water. These currents help the fish get where they're going using much less energy than they would if each fish were swimming alone—it's kind of like riding a continuous wave!

ATLANTIC HERRING

Lives in: The North Atlantic

Cool fish features: Herring get all A's when it comes to schooling. Their schools have been known to stretch 3 miles (4.8 km) across. That's more than four billion fish!

INFO BUBBLE
Misbehavior isn't limited to human schools. Fish are constantly trying to get to the middle of their schools, where it's safer, and they chase and nip at each other to get the best spot. Sounds kind of like your lunch line, huh?

Atlantic herring

Macaroni School

mini **Quest**

How hard is it for a predator to pick out a single fish from a swirling, twisting, and turning crowd? Try this Mini-Quest and see for yourself!

1. Take a handful of macaroni and drop it into a pot or bowl of water.

2. Stir the water to make a whirlpool and see if you can follow the path of a single piece of macaroni.

3. Add in another handful and try again—is it even harder now? That's what it's like for a predator to pick out one "student" in any school!

Words from the Water Wise

MARINE BIOLOGIST
Dr. Andy Rosenberg

Dr. Andy Rosenberg works at the University of New Hampshire, where he teaches and researches.

Meet **Dr. Andy Rosenberg**, a marine biologist who works on *resource management*. That means he makes sure that fish, mammals, and fishermen can all thrive while sharing the same part of the ocean. He's been an adviser on resource management to countries like the United States, Ireland, and Iceland.

Can herring reproduce fast enough to make up for the numbers that are caught? Dr. Rosenberg tries to answer questions like this.

Question: What causes some species of fish to become endangered, while others don't?

Answer: The biggest problem for fish is too much fishing. Many species can't reproduce fast enough to keep up. Other big problems for many species, especially for those that spend some of their lives in fresh water, are the loss of habitat and clean areas for reproducing and growing.

Q: What do you do to help get and keep fish off the endangered list?

A: I do research to understand the effect of changing habitat on the health of fish populations. I help provide advice to decision-makers in government on how much fishing certain populations can take and still remain healthy.

Q: What's your favorite kind of fish to study?

A: I don't know that I have a favorite fish. They're all interesting, because even though we share the Earth with them and 70 percent of the globe is covered by water, we still know very little about each species that lives in the ocean.

Q: What part of the world has the healthiest oceans and fish populations?

A: The Antarctic Ocean is probably the healthiest (because no people live there). The most endangered is around the coasts of mainland Europe and the continental United States.

Q: What can kids do to help keep the oceans healthy?

A: Learn about the ocean. What you do on land really matters to the health of the ocean. If you dump paint down the drain or spill oil or gasoline on the ground, it ends up in the ocean and contributes to pollution. If you like to fish, great, but how about releasing fish alive after you catch them? You can learn how to do this so you can have the fun of fishing without killing fish. And most important, remind your parents that you want there to be a healthy ocean when you grow up. Urge them to be careful and treat the oceans with respect.

41

Mighty Migrators

Sea Quest

Here's one you probably haven't heard:

Question: Why did the eel cross the ocean?

Answer: To eat on the other side!

Silver eels are just one of many kinds of fish that travel miles through the ocean to eat and breed. You'll find the silver eel along with some other real marathon migrators below—can you figure out where they travel?

What You Need

- 5 different colored pencils (a regular pencil is okay, too)
- Your brain

What You Do

1. Read about each fish below, then draw the path of its migration based on the clues. Use a different colored pencil for each fish.
2. Once you have all the paths drawn, find out which of these five fish swims past the most continents on its tour through the ocean. You can check all your answers on page 48.

Chinook Salmon

1. I'm born in fresh water, but during my first year of life I travel downstream and adapt to the salty ocean.
2. I swim over toward one of the biggest countries in the world, but I don't "rush in" to it.
3. Then I cross the ocean back to my birthplace.

Southern Bluefin Tuna

1. I leave Africa and swim directly east, searching for food along the way.
2. G'day mate! I'm in luck. The first continent I ran into was a beauty. I think I'll lay my eggs in the tropical waters off the southern coast.
3. Time to head home now—it's been a great trip!

Sea the Point?

As you can see from drawing these migration paths, some fish travel amazing distances around the world. But scientists are still trying to understand where they go—and *why*. Fortunately, new technology has made things easier. Today, when scientists catch a fish they want to learn more about, they attach a transmitter to it. The transmitter sends signals back to their computers, allowing the scientists to follow the fish wherever it goes.

And not long ago, scientists discovered a small bone inside the ear of a fish that contains a growth ring for each day of its first six months of life. Each ring contains information about the water chemistry from wherever the fish swam that day, which will help scientists find out exactly where in the world's waters the fish spent its time!

Silver Eel

1. When I'm just a baby, the Gulf Stream carries me up the coast of the United States and across the Atlantic to a country known for its fish and chips.
2. I transform into a transparent "glass eel" and wait for the rivers to warm up. When they do, I swim inland.
3. If I'm lucky enough not to get caught by fishermen, I'll turn around after about ten years and head back where I came from.

Monkfish

1. Brrr! It's freezing where I'm from. Time to head south for the winter!
2. *Hola!* I think I've found the coast for me. I hear there's a great city called Madrid just south of here.
3. When the cold weather leaves, so do I. Time to enjoy the summer back home!

Blue Shark

1. I'll start heading north—I'll stick close to land for now.
2. I head east at the land of maple leafs—it's getting too cold!
3. Next I swim down the coast of the continent where Christopher Columbus began his famous sea voyage. After that, I continue south, swimming along the west coast of a continent where more than 1,000 languages are spoken!
4. Time to ride the currents west and go back home!

PART 5:
The Weird and Wild!

So, ocean explorer, you're almost at the end of your journey into the wide world of fish. You've encountered *lots* of weird and wild wonders, but now it's time to enter the realm of the weirdest and wildest of all. Get ready to meet fish that spit at spiders...fish that walk...and even fish that fly!

MUDSKIPPER

Lives in:
Muddy banks of coastal swamps

Cool fish features:
This fish can walk on land—or *mud*, in this case! The mudskipper crawls out of tide pools using its bottom fins like a pair of stubby legs. Then it scurries around on the muddy surface, eating insects and looking for mates.

ARCHER FISH

Lives in:
The Asian Pacific

Cool fish features:
Archer fish are famous for their ability to shoot down insects and other small prey by spitting jets of water at them. Archer fish slip their snouts above the surface and can hit a target up to 5 feet (1.5 m) away!

Parrotfish like the one shown here can change from female to male!

PARROTFISH

Lives in: The Atlantic Ocean

Cool fish features: Wrasses like this parrotfish have a cool trick: They can switch genders! Each male wrasse lives with a group of five or six females (which he fiercely protects). If the male should die, the females don't go looking for a new guy—instead the biggest female in the group changes gender and takes over! Other fish have this gender-bending ability, too—like the clown fish you met on page 26.

Would you belive this parrotfish is actually sleeping?

Words from the Water Wise

MARINE BIOLOGIST
Dr. Robert Warner

Wonder what it's like to dive in and study fish right where they live? Then meet **Dr. Robert Warner**, a marine biologist who does just that.

Dr. Warner investigates all sorts of questions about how fish behave, like how they choose mates and how they take care of their young. He focuses a lot on fish in coral reefs, and on keeping fish populations healthy. Read on to find out about his discoveries!

Dr. Warner loves diving among colorful fish in coral reefs.

Question: You've spent a lot of time studying how fish are as parents. What have you discovered?

Answer: First, you need to know that in fish, it's mostly the males that take care of the young. We've learned that females can be very choosy about who the father will be. If a mother fish doesn't think the real father of the eggs will do a good job taking care of them (some will even eat the eggs!), she'll choose another male instead to tend to the nest.

Q: What is it about coral reefs that makes the fish that live in them so interesting?

A: Mostly, it's the vibrant colors and the unusual behaviors of animals that don't hide from you. When you're swimming among fish in a coral reef, it's like birdwatching in the tropics—but you can fly!

Q: What do you think the fish are thinking when they see human divers approach them?

A: Depends on the fish. Eating-sized fish often hide, from experience. Small fish ignore us—that's why we watch them. And very big predators—well, I don't like to imagine what they might be thinking.

Q: Have you ever been scared while on an undersea dive?

A: Mostly, it's too interesting to be scared. Once, though, on a night dive, my partner (the one with the light) disappeared just as I ran out of air AND I discovered I was tangled in seaweed. I reared back, convinced that this was my last heroic effort, and discovered I was in 2 feet (60 cm) of water!

Q: What kinds of discoveries do you hope to make about fish in the future?

A: We're working on ways to trace the paths that tiny fish larvae take from their birthplace to the place they'll spend most of their lives. As it turns out, each fish larva has a tiny piece of shell-like material in its head that tells it which way is up. That particle grows along with the fish, and we hope to use it as sort of a flight recorder to tell us where a particular young fish has been, all the way back to when it was inside its mom.

45

Who Am I?

What You Need
- Your sea smarts

The nine fish you see on the right are all strong contenders for the title of "weirdest fish in the sea." What are their names, and what *exactly* makes each one special? You'll have to figure that out yourself!

What You Do

Look at the fish photos on the next page and see if you can match each one with the right description below. You can check your answers on page 48.

1. **Glass perch:** If you've ever wanted to take a look inside a real, live fish, I'm the one for you—my body's clear, so you can see my bones while I'm still alive and swimming!

2. **Leafy seadragon:** I do everything I can to look like the seaweed I live in. I even sway around in the ocean currents like seaweed does.

3. **Trumpet fish:** I trick my prey by blending in with the scenery around me. When I dart down to suck up a small fish, it never knows what hit it.

4. **Black swallower:** I have a stomach so huge, I can eat fish twice my size!

5. **Batfish:** You'll find me standing around on the ocean floor. That's right, *standing*—I use my fins to stand up and walk around on the seafloor!

6. **Remora:** I use the top of my flat head as a suction cup to catch a ride with sharks, manta rays, and other big fish, and then I eat their leftovers.

7. **Flying fish:** I escape predators by swimming to the surface with such force that I'm propelled into the air, where I use my wing-shaped fins to soar up to 330 feet (100 m) away.

8. **Male jawfish:** I'm a really good dad. I keep eggs warm in my mouth for five to seven days, occasionally spitting them out and quickly sucking them back in to clean out any debris, give them some air, and mix up the embryos so that they develop equally.

9. **Parrotfish:** I spend an hour before bedtime spinning a slimy sleeping bag made of mucous to keep me safe from predators.

Fishing for More?

Okay, ocean explorer, it's time to close up these fish files and swim back to the surface. But does that mean you've seen your last leafy seadragon? Your final frogfish? Hope not! You'll keep finding plenty of great fish like these throughout your time at Undersea U. And, depending on where you live or vacation, you could even plan a visit to an aquarium or a natural history museum to get an even closer look at your favorite fish.

And remember—your imagination can be home to lots more wild species. Just dig into your Make-Your-Own Fish Kit and piece together your own undersea sensations! And for even more fish-designing fun, make sure to stop by **www.scholastic.com/undersea**!

So, until next month, keep fishing for more *fun*-dersea adventures!

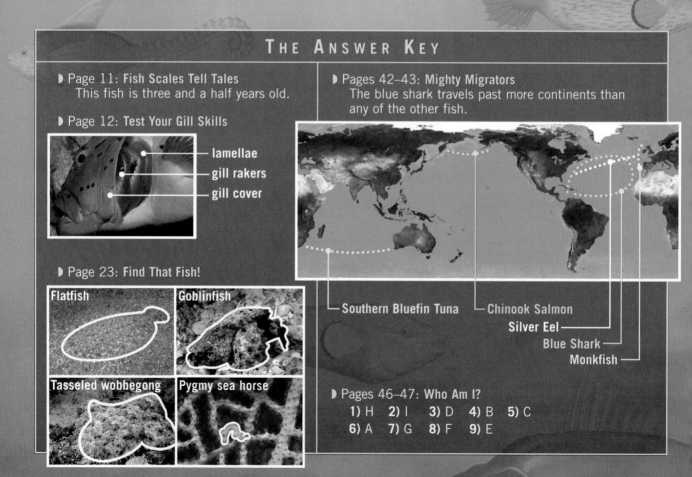

THE ANSWER KEY

▶ **Page 11: Fish Scales Tell Tales**
This fish is three and a half years old.

▶ **Page 12: Test Your Gill Skills**
- lamellae
- gill rakers
- gill cover

▶ **Page 23: Find That Fish!**

Flatfish

Goblinfish

Tasseled wobbegong

Pygmy sea horse

▶ **Pages 42–43: Mighty Migrators**
The blue shark travels past more continents than any of the other fish.

Southern Bluefin Tuna — Chinook Salmon
Silver Eel
Blue Shark
Monkfish

▶ **Pages 46–47: Who Am I?**
1) H   2) I   3) D   4) B   5) C
6) A   7) G   8) F   9) E